SONGS
FROM
THE SHADOWS

POEMS

by

Lamont L. Nance

Songs from the Shadows

Copyright 2019 by Lamont L. Nance

Published by the Green Thrush Press
Box 431, Yellow Springs, Ohio

Printed in the United States of
America

ISBN- 9781696748445

Dedication

I dedicate this book to my Grandmother,

Gladys Mae.

This road is very long without you.

Meow man!

Lamont L. Nance

Praise for *Songs from the Shadows*

"Indeed, reading this provocative collection of Lamont Nance's poetry is to experience, 'your emotions racing like missiles in your veins' (*Remembrance Lost*). These pages of sharp humor and blunt introspection, like holding vigil, are cause for deep breath and a pause that is near to the sacred, fragile as a blue jay's broken wing and ponderously bold as an epic journey to know why. Alone, each poem is a wonder; gathered together, they reveal the rare gift of a remarkable man, strong and courageous enough to be vulnerable and honest enough to give us a human story both pained and hopeful. It was a humbling grace to first hear the voice of these poems read to me from a yellow legal pad, words and lines scratched into their own cadence during so many night hours shared in a prison cell. It is an honor to commend to you such a poignant song from the shadows." ~ B. Burnside, former Lutheran Bishop; contributing author, *Hear My Voice: A Prison Prayer Book*

"From over a decade of prison experience,

Lamont Nance has created a rich and riveting tapestry of prison life and a reminder of what we miss when we lock people away. This kind of writing, full of life and hope and love, teaches us some of the lessons we so desperately need to learn." ~ R. Rubin, College Counselor

"Nance's poetry lets us in, lets us feel his world, lets us live, for a time, in his days. His descriptions of the most everyday of daily situations disabuse us of the notion that the imagination and heart can be imprisoned. It is a glimpse of a narrative to which too few of us have access, and for which I am grateful. " ~ D. Witte, School Administrator

"Lamont Nance has a furtive and fertile imagination and the will and urgency to allow it wide range in his poetry. Deeply felt and deeply affecting, his words are clearly his sanctuary. *Songs from the Shadows* demonstrates the power of experience to open and transform; the poems are, in Lamont's words, like "finding newly wrapped gifts every time I wake up." ~ L. Newman, retired university adviser

"I was inspired and encouraged to read Lamont Nance's *Songs from the Shadows*. This poet's ideas and images rise free above his environment to inspire us and call us to action. His is a talent to be cherished, nurtured, and encouraged." ~ J. M. Davis, retired professor

"Lamont Nance takes "demons of the past" and "devils of the future" and makes them work as intimate and generous poetry. An insightful, fierce and original voice from behind the walls. he shares a discomforting message in a genuine and powerful voice." ~ A. O'Connor, data analyst

"Lamont's poems are bracing: They capture the tension between the hope that sustains him and the experiences of isolation and loneliness that can define life in prison. Heartbreaking, authentic, and unblinking, Nance's poetry gives us a lesson in survival and in the transformative power of a trustworthy and generous spirit. *Songs from the Shadows* will give heart to all who read it." ~ R. M. Felker, retired administrator

"The poems in this collection are complex for different reasons; they require the reader to take time to attend to all that is going on: literary references, juxtaposition of experiences, imaginative allusions. Nance uses a light touch and we are left to contemplate the views he gives us – of fear and faith, grief and curiosity – and above all – appreciation. " ~ L. Morningstar, English teacher

Acknowledgments

With any endeavor, there must be belief for it to blossom into hope. Hope for something better. To be better. A road from hope to love. Love that many of us don't feel we're worthy of in some ways. Especially me. But we are. And it leaves us wondering, how do you thank people for something so precious? You cannot. Yet, I believe now, you can just live in gratitude and strive to live up to the love. Even when you stumble, because the beauty of Love is that it is the Sun rising in the East.

I want to thank my mentor, Patricia, for

teaching me how to love for the sake of loving. I owe you a lot, my dear. My life coach, Mary Lou, thank you for for all the stern advice and those swift kicks back to reality. I need them from you, Sister. Francisco and Gabriela, I cannot thank you enough because I am beyond grateful for your friendship and understanding. It means more than you know.

To my brother, Bruce - senor sideburn – for all the late nights and endurance through these fraught years. For being my best friend, big brother, and bringing shade into my life. For the tears of hardship and for the joy you salvaged. Thank you for everything.

Thank you to Janna, Jody, Jill, Jenny, and Jim for embracing me in your own ways and welcoming a stranger into your lives on the strength of the love you have for my brother. Thank you for carrying him far. Love begets love, right?

A special thank you to Roberta and to her brother, Bill, whose time and talent and willingness to work with the Amazon format made this book manifest. And thanks to Ann, who also gave her efforts and time to this project.

To my family – too many of you wombats to name! You know who you are! My mother, SaRai, for reminding me of the Sun – your love is brilliance itself. Thank you, my Earth. My siblings,

Kristina, Jasmine, and Stanley – I love you. It's been hard but we're all we've got! My Uncles Ike and Legs, the heroes who never knew they were. Your strength strengthens me. My Aunt Twanda, I love you, baby! You are indeed a Southern bombshell. My children: Ja'Quan, Brantavius, and Amayha, thank you for never disbelieving. Thank you for loving me all these long years. I love you more than life.

I sincerely think this book belongs to all of you.

About the Author

Lamont L. Nance is a Midwestern boy, all the way through. Born in Chicago, Illinois and raised in Milwaukee, Wisconsin, he has a vast love for Lake Michigan. He is an avid reader, a deep thinker, and a lover of anything Manga-related. He lives in Black River Falls, Wisconsin – for now. This is his first book of poetry.

Lamont L. Nance

TABLE OF CONTENTS

A Glance a Poem

I saw you this morning half awake, sloshing
coffee around and chomping a bagel. Late.
Deadlines to meet and a million things to do
10 minutes ago. But your gas tank is full
and there is no traffic. God bless the little
things.

Lamont L. Nance

A Question

When you look to the sky on dismal days,

Do you imagine the sun shines for you,

That shadows of trees are waiting to dance

with you,

Or before you sleep that the stars dim?

Lamont L. Nance

A Song from the Shadows

There is a cadence if you choose to listen,

A chant to align echoing across ages to

attune

To earth, to ancestors, to the Universe

willing you forward,

From the umbra to help find the resonance,

For the key that opens the door of

continuous soul;

If you listen like your life depends upon it,

You will find that voice thought alien and

foreign,

Discover that you are integral to this human

choir.

Lamont L. Nance

A Stone No Longer

Here I've sat for millennia uncounted.

Ensconced within the incorporeal scars of
memories lost;

a telling too vast to be written

and not empty enough to be full.

Here I've watched ages come and go

as life brachiated and grew plentiful;

colorful as a field of flowers

and more beautiful than the dead of night.

Here I've felt a multitude of expression;

driven beyond the turbid depths of joy

and the ecstatic crescendo of wrath.

Here I've known succor and disparagement;

made sense of the laconic

and rationalized insanity.

Here I've fought the Great Eroder in a battle

where I've died a billion times over.

And so here I lie,

a bed of sand.

Alas, I am a stone no longer.

Almost We Were There

Almost we were there. Inside that grand palace upon the mountain drifting in the heavens. You and I eating that divine ambrosia amongst the colonnades. Almost. We were there. Hedonistic in our immortality, brightened by youth. Living only for the moment of our fragile existence. Almost. We were there. On the brink of equanimity and societal understanding of the human essence. Learning to deviate from the lurking hatred of our baser selves. Almost we were there. So close to obtaining the equipoise of a rational mind. But it was not to be.

Almost. We were there. Before we threw

away all reason and death became our ruler. Before all hell broke loose and parricide became the mores of the homicidally inclined. Almost we were there. Pompous in our greed for power; so eager to destroy that which made us what we are. Stagnant at the point of ascension and the gods of old were nearly dethroned. Almost. We were there. Ignorant of the balance of all things and what we were meant to be. Eviscerating ourselves instead of becoming more. Almost. We were there. Nearly there. But being content wasn't enough.

Am and Am Not

Reality defined descriptively is realer than real. It's over burdening. The only thing heavier than that is the air I breathe. So, I don't. My name is Mountain. I hold up the sky. Anyone who has ever felt and carried that type of weight understands. Women. Slaves. The underestimated.

I am light. I am dense. I am present. Sentinel. Witness my stoic visage in its brachiated understanding of what isn't important; how it shifts as snow blankets the imperfection of perspective. Witness that I *carry.* I am an environment my own. A part of. Separate from. Earth. The Womb.

Listen to the leaves and you will hear the thoughts of rivers and, ultimately, the deep thoughts of oceans and seas. But not mine. Mine are akin to that of space … empty and vastly full; unimaginable, yet longed to be understood like that soft ache unrequited despite the seasons. But thoughts are just emotions and feelings given flesh. Identity. Action. Who we assume we are.

I am nothing and everything. A notion. Just form stationary believed to be stagnant since movement became obsolete. My roots are deep, my vision shallow and glorious as clouds in the false dawn.

I am Duty. I am Loss. I am Love in every facet of your humanity. I am not any of those things. I am that silence in your ears

when the house is vacant and the heart-line
seems weak. I'm just being. Nothing more
than that.

Try it some time.

Lamont L. Nance

Avow

To be your best friend – even if you're sick
of me.

To remind you of your worth – whenever
you feel you don't matter.

To not be vacant when things get hard – I
will not run away from you.

To listen to you even when it hurts to – you
will never be unheard.

To love you to the moon and back – when
you can't love yourself.

To remember why, when the sun sets – the
morning will answer itself.

To never give up on you – when passion's
magma cools and euphoria's gas clears.

I vow to hold your hand always.

Lamont L. Nance

Being Adult

Do tell me everything quickly

So that I learn nothing as fast

Damn, shoulda listened in class

Lamont L. Nance

Beware the Bad Guy

I am footprints upon air

Disenchanted for the sake of propriety

For self

Anointed by me and encouraged by I

I am the dust of crushed bones

Cloying

Thick like babies' breath

Winterized for general purposes

Ride my wavelength

Discover the Dragon within

I breaststroke through magma for levity

Breathe sulfur to clear my mind

Drink saltwater to lighten me up

Eat oysters glazed with cyanide to clear me out

I'm as pure as space, fossilized by the cosmos

I am the BAD GUY

What the best writers ineptly convey at their best

Displacement finalized

I have chosen to create

Brought universes into existence

Destroyed them in boredom to eat their remains

I am fearless

I challenge you to be the same.

Bird on the Ground

Every morning I have this routine. Shower. Brush teeth. Drink tea. Eat waffles with lots of peanut butter and syrup. Walk the bike trail. This is my routine. Every day. Every. Single. Day. From 4:41 to 6:21 every morning for the last nine years. No deviation or hiccups. It is the single constant in my existence. During this time I prepare myself for the world, observe the rise of humanity before the workday begins, and relish the sentient blossoming of the Earth as the Sun ascends. In this I find communion.

Today was no different ... at first. One hour and seventeen minutes into my walk, something beautiful and tragic stopped me in my tracks. I could not go past. I couldn't retrace my steps. That hesitancy forced me to really question why I held onto this routine and why I did not hold more in this life dear.

There on the ground was a bird. A Blue Jay. Its left wing hung awkwardly. It was broken. All the chirps and tweets it emitted were pain-filled. A song of dissonance that mirrored the one in my heart. It wriggled and flap-hopped counter clock-wise before stopping, breathing heavily in apparent agony. On its last turn, a beady, intelligent eye regarded me as I watched it. Neither the bird nor I breathed for an instant.

My thoughts were as sand in an hourglass.

Questions breached and then filled my mind as torrential rain tends to flood. What if a feral cat or coyote happened upon it? What if an early morning trekker ran it over while cycling? What if it starved to death? What would be its fate if I had not walked today? Dread built in my core. There are too many dangers in the world for a flightless bird whose sole means of evasion is its ability to fly.

Someone has to save it, I remember thinking. But why me? Those words raged, a banshee wronged, swirled and swirled like a tornado. Then, almost unbidden, the response! Why not me? What I felt was more than just because there was no one else there. No, it was far more. Why not the boy who stumbled along through life just as broken as the bird before me? Why not save something when it couldn't save itself? Because…because I wasn't saved by a world that demands bloodlessly tight boots and the self-reliance to level a mountain. Alone.

Because I needed saving and no one ever came.

A chasm opened up within the silence that descended. A shift transpired in me. I couldn't differentiate myself from the bird. My vision narrowed, grew displaced, and before I understood my action, the bird was in my hands. A strange warbling filled the air. Something leaked from my nose and cheeks itched. I could barely see where I was going.

The sound of traffic, the screeching of tires and the honking of horns brought me out of my inconsolable reverie. A taxi glowed like a light from Heaven. We got in and I kindly told the driver where to go. One thing I will never forget was how, through it all, the Blue Jay didn't move the least bit within my fragile grasp.

Lamont L. Nance

Black Man

Black Man

You were killed for protecting yourself.

Black Man

You were slayed running with your hands in

the air.

Black Man

You were murdered on your wedding day –

your car looked like Swiss cheese.

Black Man

You were decimated for striding proudly –

the excuse was standing their ground.

Black Man

Momma watched your breath stop when you

failed to reach her in time.

Black Man

You were shot in the back – why are they

afraid of you?

Black Man

Your light can never be stolen – you, the

Sun, you are not a candle to be snuffed out.

Brother

Remember the good feelings when the arduous is everything you know.

Remember the embrace that soothed your core as the reactor of your passion's meltdown.

Remember the love in those eyes and the knowing of their depths in times of shallow indifference.

Remember the sound of that voice when the silence of empty walls echoes volumes in your mind.

Remember.

Remember.

Keep in mind a reason that warms as a coal protected in winter.

Don't forget the taste of joy.

Keep in mind those shadeless days upon the heart.

Don't forget why you choose to love.

Remember.

Remember.

Remember the significance of water at the edge of a most cherished

Place among pines and spruce.

Remember, Brother, that all of those things are still yours and that they will never leave you.

Candle Dark

This aching light, a blossomed sun within this darkened room, reminds me of the fragility of all things. How all can be ensconced and wisped away permanently. For in this moment, I fear that in the morning I won't remember your face as it is now. Ethereal. Heart-wrenching. Disheveled haired. Face pillow lined without make up. *Lovely.*

Please, stay still as you are looking at me with a curious wonderment at the intent of my gaze. A heart beat … an intake of air. And there, briefly, a vulnerable expectancy to the curve of your lips as you smile shyly at me. So beautiful … the way the light catches the hollow of your throat, heightens the prominence of your cheekbones and makes your pert nose desirable in ways I hadn't noticed until now.

So full this space, this instance, with you that there is no room to breathe; too hard to not feel you pressed against me an arm's length away. No. Don't come any further, please. Let your heart cross to meet mine in this dark uncertainty, brightened only by that candle upon the table across the room.

Capitalism

I'll trade you two Now and Laters

For half your Snickers bar

And then trade that for a Twinkie.

Swap the Twinkie for a bag of Doritos,

Exchange the Doritos for a Pepsi.

Sell the Pepsi for two dollars because it's the

last one,

Buy three Honeybuns for a dollar and

pocket the other.

Distribute the Honeybuns for a Washington

each. Now I've got four and I'll quadruple

that to sixteen.

Since you want my five year-old bomber

jacket

Seventeen dollars … I'll put away six and

buy two

Five dollar pizzas and sell all sixteen slices
for two

Bucks and a pop after the game.

Now I'm at thirty-two ... so I double up

And buy four more pizzas and sell at the
same rate next week.

Sixty-four smackeroos quicker than a sneeze

Spend forty on a used Ipod and sell it to you
for sixty

Because yours broke last week when you
dropped it.

My next is a Franklin and two but I got an
old

HEMAN action figure you've been dying
for and

I'm not selling for less than two hundred.

Isn't it sweet what two Now and Laters can
do?

But don't tell the IRS.

Caretakers

Nietzsche had a mountain and thunderclouds

to amuse

I lurk chasms and abysmal stars that

refuse

Within myself without myself there is

Frost

I quest that murky ocean of what is

lost

Reaching beyond the tide for

Rumi

To dance upon that road of daggers

with me

Waiting for the comfort of a

Packard

Behind the wheel with my friend,

Mr. Stafford

To remember that silence in self is to be

awake

That I might transcend this plane along with

Blake

In winter, I'm reminded of life by

Oliver

For within those pages she gave

all of her

By paying close attention to the song of

Whitman

I understood the different facets of being

man

In my bitter-most hours I learned of faith

from R.M.R.*

I've been transfigured by it all so now I have

no bar

*Rainer Maria Rilke

Contingencies

If "if" were a fifth

We'll be drunk as a skunk

Does anyone have bail money?

Lamont L. Nance

Cotillion

Today I saw shadows dance

The fire burned it all down

Except for the shadows

They continued to dance

And revealed too much

I wish it never started

Lamont L. Nance

Darker Side of the Moon

Light up what came before

Not to erase or cover up

Nor to invite a hollowness in spirit

Witness beauty blacker and bleaker

Than the darkest of paths

Man will ever take

The stigma refined

For a filament within

Reclamation of the enlivened

Commonality in shards

Of satellites dislodged

And vacancies unfulfilled…

To burn a universe pure

Down and dismantled

Softly fit and deft

Connect the piece that doesn't

Somewhere believed to be lost

Vile in its absence

An umbra regard pitted

With avarice resigned

To embrace the untouchable

And attain voidance

Upon a precipice to stand

To observe nebulas forevermore

Fashioned incompletely

In tune and discordant

Alas, a bitter smile to please

Everything Possible

Perhaps a step will be all that is needed

To cross that bridge

To mend what thought unmendable

Maybe a step can change the unchangeable

Lamont L. Nance

Fecundity

My anger deserted me

That sweltering maelstrom

Quaker of tectonics

Displacer of space

That volition demanding

Existence which seethed

As I journeyed into

The void of myself

Such wrath to devastate

Slash and break and rip

Gone

Gone cold to still a heart

In a flimsy breath gone

Why do I feel so empty?

Lamont L. Nance

Feeling Up-Pity

In completing a task we tend to use what is in reach. When we eat, we use our hands, a fork, a knife or a spoon. These things are interchanged without thought. We are taught to work smarter and not harder so we go through life like broken records and disregard harmony. Utilizing a maul when situations require a chisel.

You cannot eat peas with a knife. Nor can a spoon part steak effectively, just as a fork isn't ideal for cereal at breakfast. Why be surprised that our edges are blunt and our words cut sharper than diamonds? When given the wrong utensils for life is it any wonder that our tables lack etiquette?

Lamont L. Nance

For Feet

Think nothing of socks today

Sandled summer for the arrival of freedom

A cool breeze to enjoy

I've gone out alone

untethered in desire

for more

becoming more.

Beyond the abyss within my chest

being the silence of the Living Quiet

hollow and hallowed.

The rapaciousness of stone

the effort of trees

benign.

I've gone out alone

walked the artic corridor

in search of peace

found nothing akin to it.

I've gone

feigning lawfulness

maintaining civility

alone.

Within the small places my chaos reigns

out there

beyond you and your godly selfhood

to see the sun never set.

Glimmer

There are no islands, just water

Miles and miles of it that reach across

Horizons walking horizons swimming them

Oceans and galaxies of water seeking

To pull under that light which buoys

The reason

There is so much water, water to choke

And instill forgetfulness and leaves you

forsaken out there in the darkness waiting

for that

Glimpse in the east to garner hope, hope

That something will change.

But swimming is all you've got.

Lamont L. Nance

Hmm…

Rosy nights do remind me

Of winter cheeks beyond summer's reach

And deep-crusted apple pies

Lamont L. Nance

Inches

Inches is a word disregarded when the hectic moments of everyday life consume us completely. Inches. How do they measure to words like feet, kilometers, miles, and yards? In comparison to years?

What can distance learn from an inch? Something so miniscule as to be dismissed? One thing or a dozen, I say. Everyone recognizes endeavors are undertaken with a single step. However, we all unconsciously ignore the incremental processes the mind grows through. In inches. Even more minute than that. What distance learns from the inch are things many of us just don't have very much of at times. Patience. Steadfastness. Forbearance. Determination. Tolerance. Of them, anything of importance is fashioned.

There is a tendency to gravitate toward the highest peak to look upon the clouds below, or to delve an oceanic trench bereft of all illumination in order to find substance. These are extremes, life comprises them, but its foundation is of inches. Our lives are <u>made</u> of them.

It is the little things that make winter gray days glow like Floridian afternoons. Weaponizes our beings to fight for what is precious to us and allocates the strength to endure. Love is <u>born</u> of that. Those inches we all forget that happen to be important. That we take for granted.

The extra smile in the morning. Doing something needed unasked. Being silent when words move like bears through a forest of wind chimes. Making a task easier

by asking: How can I help you? Saying I
love you for nothing at all in the oddest
moments.

These are inches and they make up a
life. Cultivate them and learn Happiness'
measure.

Lamont L. Nance

In Love with Her Solitude

I'm enchanted.
She lounges in repose, reading within a
world her own
Transfixed upon a precipice of literary
enlightenment.
I take furtive glances – doing my best not to
stare:
Such peace of self within that silence --
it cannot be viewed as introversion
but taken as eloquence in action.
Oh, how I love her solitude.

Our words are riveting and companionable,
Like great oaks a hundred yards apart –
with just the sound of the wind and bristling
leaves

Within a sigh or the gentle bowing of

branches unrequited

The turn of a page, the slightest shift in a

chair

A multitude of expression.

I am in love with her solitude.

Isn't It Obvious

One day you'll regret those long pauses

Which turn into silences that birth distance

One day there will be regret for not reaching

out

When kind words aren't meant to be held

back

One day can be all that matters between two

hearts

Between eyes of despair and eyes of joy

One day will come where the simple flexing

Of a few muscles and twinkling eyes won't

heal the wounds one day

Just one day

Isn't it obvious one day won't be there to

regret

Because one day you'll meet death?

Why is it so hard then?

Just in Case

When the pall of uselessness blankets us –

be super. Be human.

Superhuman?

I guess what I'll try to express to you is

remembrance.

Everyday try to remember – we ball

unpleasantness up and stuff it within a box

to be displaced a universe away.

We run away.

We run to make believe anything other than

this:

This current shape our lives have grown

into.

Remember … you.

Remember why you've come so far, why

you've never given up

And continued to love anyway… even when

you're right to hate.

Remember to be kind.

Especially to yourself because our world is

brutal,

Often blatantly inconsiderate, and ignorant

of the truth that

We're all living for love.

A warm bed in winter.

Food. Peace of mind.

Remember this just in case you find yourself

disbelieving that some people are even

human.

Kill Them with Kindness

I am the APEX. I drag my monsters with me to the killing fields of fear, that beast of wrack, to meet my demons of the past and my devils of the future. They have haunted and taunted me for eons. No more. I have come to kill.

But they never die. Every weapon known to man, imagined and unimagined, I have used to no avail. Mass destruction and extinction level event are preschool terms for the devastation left behind.

I have drunk the blood of the Old Gods, armed and armored myself beyond the conceivable in preparation, before bathing

within the fires of Creation. I emerged with
a multiverse in my mind and godlings within
my veins; to bleed existence into existence
in my wake.

I AM THE APEX AND IT ALL
RESEMBLES A FILAMENT OF THE
THREAD OF THE FABRIC OF WHICH
NONE ARE CENTRAL!

Upon those fields I found them gloriously
profane, their eyes thirsting to…to feel
anything. So, I hugged each and every last
one of them, because they needed it more
than I ever had.

Lament Nothing

I have always known hardship,

Understood each step was blistering,

Every precipice a choice of razor,

Having witnessed nothing but desolation;

My heart shown only desert,

My mind displaced in the bleakness,

My soul forsaken for errors not my own,

For an oasis I'm never allowed to visit;

For a blame sought in fear of silence,

I have known no thing of good,

Not a genuine laugh heard in forever,

For all the miles walked for some thing;

And the time lost in the wait,

Grant me the mantle of the night,

Give me the succor of the cold,

Show me nothing but what is consistent;

In the least I know what to expect of you,

Pardon my back.

Lifting the Bucket

Tiredness seeps deeply when I view the path back. It is longer than previous experience. Ice encrusted branches of the Great Oak shine like a million unreachable stars within a Moon lit universe. A chill breeze re-avows its everlasting sorrow, and on this winter's night, I cannot ignore my own.

Snow has become tightly packed inside the crevasses of the salted cobblestones leading to my house. My elbows ache from bringing up the pail. My feet are cold because in my haste to return, I spilled the frosty water into my boots. And I don't want to move.

And I hurt. Hurt because Life, itself, demands change and growth whether you accept it or not. Whether it is good or bad. It doesn't matter if its concepts and notions are beyond our understanding. Our opinions and assertiveness hold no water. And there is *nothing* more frightening to a human being than discovering you don't matter.

Often, I wonder what drives us on despite how ... *bleak* it can all be. Is it defiance? The frantic clawings of the Ego? Faith? Love of another? The first footsteps of a child? The grasp of a hand while times are dire? Self-preservation? Hatred? *Or,* could it be the lies we live by?

I waste time, out here, standing in the

cold contemplating things I cannot answer. I will never know the most concise one since everything is mutable – with one's perception and understanding. What I know is that this well dug up by my great great great great grandfather's Uncle will be here after I'm gone. Perhaps long after. What I do know is that my toes are cold and it is warmer in the house, where people who believe in me are awaiting my return. I know that I'm going to lift this bucket and go inside.

Lamont L. Nance

Looking at the Moon

When words come to mind as I think of you
It is easy to grow esoteric as concepts amass
to define
Explaining a depth that isn't within and isn't
without is hard.

Yet to await … held within breath
Ephemeral as a step through shadows
Brilliant galaxies are but a flowing of
corridors – leading to you.
I guess I can mix and match
In order to stitch together what is left
A life – that pause before the inhale; a heart.

Still the cold unrelents
Beautiful explosions, eons away, give life

through surrender

Novas are space bees pollinating the

universe of love.

Without exception you accept

Hands – a caress beyond this mortal form

Leaving sanctity in the dusting of your

touch.

Nothing but that face construed upon the

darker side

Jagged, pitted, scarred, and lighter than all it

satiates

Illumined – eclipsing the sun's heart.

Who is the moon? You? Me?

Who is the earth? One is bound to the other

either way.

To orbit is to observe to observe is to behold

– I am stunned.

Love Poem

Ha!

What do words matter anyway

When love is a ready hot cup

In the morning?

Lamont L. Nance

Marching Horses

I am the devastation wrought when powers

converge

A blade scaled of the darkest edge

unsheathed

I am War: give me your blood and misery

I am the darkness in your heart when your

humanity falters

Witness the air around me explode in

response

I am Famine: I am what you can never have

I am the verge manifested beyond the

inchoate

The sinister rift warping the world in my

wake

I am Pestilence: embrace this euphoric rot

I am the void, the sentinel, the cosmic

overlord

The cold to burst trees, the cold that scours

souls

I am Death: your efforts are nothing

Misconception

I can't think of anything more embarrassing
than dribbling piss on the front of your
pants. Perhaps leaving the bathroom with
toilet paper hanging from the back of your
pants is more so. Or finding out that I was
wrong about you....

Lamont L. Nance

Moments in Stasis

We race up and down the stairs headlong

Our minds sponges within partisan

fishbowls

Filled with conditions made human by

default

Praying nothing shatters our film of denial

Ignoring the ocean existing outside us

To keep those breaths inhaled that unname

Every hopeful reason to light that first fire

Lamont L. Nance

Necessity's Ignominy

Yard bird, you were taken away by hands of
desperation in greed for salvation. Your
wings clipped—feathers plucked because
they were beautiful. Your life bagged and
made nothing in an instant; the time your
parents spent together discovering love—
their embrace in the fashioning of you made
irrelevant.

You were gutted, seasoned, and filled with
candied raisins. Eaten by people that never
loved you. I am so sorry, but you made a
terrific sandwich.

Lamont L. Nance

No Longer

I no longer search

because I already have the world

I no longer have a name

because the land is my name

I no longer listen to the wind

because the chimes whistle underwater

I no longer wish to obtain

because time isn't on my side

I no longer participate

because I have no reason to compete

I no longer watch for spring

because in my heart it is perpetual

no longer do you have to read this poem

because it makes no sense and it's almost

Lamont L. Nance

Nostalgia

Give me crisp air and warm pie

Wandering mornings and secluded nights

Fire pits and deep fried turkey

Football games and silly parades

On Thanksgiving Day just give me family

Lamont L. Nance

Notions Upon a Lake

When I think of Lake Michigan, I often
view it as a vast, gray, roiling receptacle that
withstood all I raged at it, like an infant
slapping its hands in bath water, that
accepted the tears that I knew were
unending and gave no solace for the sorrow
which consumed my being. It did nothing.
Just lapped at the rocks with a lassitude that
made me question why I ever went back to it
ever again. It was harsh in its solemnity.

But it was there for me in a fashion that no
one had ever been. Called me back with its
solitude and made me understand what that
meant in its unrelenting silence. My anger

and pain meant nothing confronting such a visage; within such an expression lies the futility we discover as children when going against our parents. We are helpless against their strength, their will, and their perception of us – in order to thrive. And so very dependent upon them, alas. To Lake Michigan, I was a child reluctant to heed sage advice and, for my petulance, it bombarded me with its deafening quietude and sullen gusts of dead fish.

I recall going to the Lake one summer afternoon and although it was bustling with people, trawling for whatever it is we're ultimately seeking in our lives, it felt empty to me and filled with a darkness I couldn't define. It was a beautiful day. There happened to be a grace that bespoke of balance and community, of safety, with shared responsibility for our fellow human beings. <u>But I felt nothing of it</u>. Desolate. I was … separate.

It was only during the midnight hour that I began to feel any semblance of interconnectedness, of understanding, and what peace may have been. What I realized, many years later, was the fact that the darkness perceived, reflected, only my limited understanding of myself and was indeed a projection of what I harbored against myself. It ate at me. I … it … we were symbiotic.

There were nights where the stars glimmered for me in ways I thought hallucinogenic, the waves queried my soul and found the answers shallow, revealed them to be the inept yearnings of a teenage boy that could not go beyond the fear of being inadequate. The Lake questioned my right to be angry, why it was important to me, my understanding of and capability to love selflessly, fed me the temporary solace a junkie received and kept me wanting more. It left me with nothing but a memory of a love I could have but never hold. Left me never being able to rest easy at night knowing that she cared.

Lake Michigan couldn't. So, I love her as she is, not for what she is not. My bastion of silence when I needed it most. My Fortress of Solitude. A bittersweet memory that will live with me forever.

Lake Michigan showed me you had to experience what it means to be alone in order to know the importance of just being there. Something that meant you may be alone afterwards, for many years, even, but you were a sentinel in a world so transitory which never recognized its passing.

Lamont L. Nance

Ode to the Offshoot of Black and White

All of my clouds are gray:

Dove, charcoal, steel, oxford,

Heather … and the gray that is grey.

Beautiful fulminations ruminating

About what new grays to

Birth into the world, as

Gray as the ocean during

A typhoon or hurricane,

Gray as I sometimes

Feel in winter, crisp and clean and

Solid and ascendant.

Mountainous grays that fill

The blood with dirty rocks

That aren't dirt but brighter than

Rainbows and fields of sunflowers.

Gray. An amazing color.

Today I am gray and I'm okay with that.

Ode to You

Walk the shadows of yourself

Be ready to cry and know fear

To doubt, going on anyway

Lamont L. Nance

Only

I'm waiting for you

Just you

The one who I've felt all these long years

Wanting to know everything

Of you

To glory in the wonder that your parents

witnessed

Discovering a new joy

Only you

Like finding newly wrapped gifts every time

I wake up

Lamont L. Nance

Parentheses

Be quick about it.

(What is the rush for?)

Be quicker yesterday.

(Why are you hurrying?)

Do it quickly now.

(How much regret will you have later?)

Lamont L. Nance

Penny

A single profile presented:

One eye, one cheek, half a nose,

Half a smile, a perfect ear,

No face at all.

Enigmatic.

Do not look to my face of leather,

Of diamond and scraps of metal

Welded together in matrimony.

Stitched.

Stapled.

Scalped and left torn flapping

Ears drawing flies buzzing for a taste.

A face to remember.

Faceless.

A single profile resented.

The contrast shifts to

Encompass the beauty it covets.

Caricatures drawn in the sand…

Money is just what we make it!

An idea.

Never underestimate the

Power of imagination.

Pictures

When silence disappears and the voice of
objectivity shatters, I turn to after-images.
They fill my mind. Woven tapestries finer
than spider-webbed vistas which remind my
soul of what is missing. Moments inhaled to
recalibrate; fostering alignment when
symmetry is hindered. To remember is to
see. See fog laboring over fields to dance
among the trees before the sun appears.

Once I received a photo depicting the
austerity of the Dead Sea. Nothing lives
there. Just gravelly shores of sand and stone.
And salt. Lots of salt. There are rocky hills
and caves where, I imagine, people have
hidden from the heat, marauders, or gone to

just be in a cave. In reality, sacred scrolls

have been found there. In my mind, if I turn

sideways, a light haze glimmers nearly

ignored by the reflection of its surface. The

sky a perfectly clear blue stretching for eons.

Sometimes after a light rain at the peace of

morning's ease, I sit with a cup of Earl Grey

to watch for birds and wonder how they

view this world. There was a picture of a

robin I happened to glimpse, showing it

about to fly. Its balance fragile, its visage

filled with certainty. When the air is heavy, I

think of that bird.

How does one describe a photo of cherry

blossoms? This is my only attempt: It is to

be lived. Breathed. Held within you as if you

can only eat color. Or gauging the love of

one looking back at you for the millionth time. Immeasurable, Fleeting Wondrous. All a facsimile.

A pathway of cobblestones extends from a cabin amidst pine and spruce, leading down toward a lake frequented by loons and turtles. I envision bonfires and laughter shared there. Think of what it must take to honor a mother's request to meet her at the dock. Imagine such a bond.

One day, I was dragging my bike inside when my mother called my name. I glanced up slack-jawed and fish-eyed in response. She took a photo. I remember feeling embarrassed and angry for being set up, because I hated having my picture taken. Now I insist on taking them whenever I can, ask others to take them when they vacation so that I can see life as they do. The irony isn't lost on me.

There is an insistence on brevity when so much of our lives is too detailed for words. Instead we rely on capturing instances to remind us when we forget them. This is a mental error. So I'll be brief. Make your life more than just a picture.

Ravages

Ignore pages of lives untold,
of memories forgotten and laughter
unshared;
no crinkles to view along the eyes,
that don't readily embrace seasons past.
No testaments endured or worth
acknowledging inside.

What is there but fragility when crashing
against rocks?
Or falling tens of thousands of feet from
your bed to the floor?
No practitioner or caretaker – just you and
the seconds before.
No deftness left – just inept signals sent in
real time that mock.

Other than receiving expediently what is
truly expected,
Should a door be partial despite the key that
fits?

Renewal

If I am nothing to you

Now that you had to let me go

Why has the silence of my steps

Reminded you of what you already know?

Lamont L. Nance

Remembrance Lost

I remember you black boy

Before you learned to fight back.

When you opened your mouth and said

nothing.

Your emotions racing like missiles in your

veins.

Practicing before the mirror to become

empty.

I remember you.

Remember when you snuck to read to

escape.

How poetry was used to cleanse your rage.

And bikes and dogs were your passion

forever.

Until it became music and cars and girls.

I remember you black boy.

The streets and alleyways walked for a
home.
When you realized that nothing you did
worked.
Remember the winter night your heart
slowly died.
And left poetry and books for a gun.
I remember you.
How your world became dark and vicious.
That shadow helped you recall the good.
By helping when nobody else was kind
enough.
You fought to remember the words inside
you.
I remember you black boy.

Resilient

I no longer worry

Because most days are a punch to the face.

And blood trickling down the throat

I don't worry about finding joy

When elbows fly and knees seek soft places

Impacts which rattle belief in non-violence

I can't worry any more

When my hands are scraped raw

To keep off the ground

So I can avoid deadly kicks

I do not worry

Since it's my turn to beat you

And I hope you can take it, Life

But I doubt it, as most abusers can't.

Lamont L. Nance

Rest of My Life

Recollect

Recollection

Recollected

Recall

Recalling

Recalled

Memory

Memories

Memorized

Images of you

To hold close

To capture you

Sweet bird

So that I can

Remember you

For the rest

Of my life

Season Ditty

Winter has aches and pains.

Spring has moody mornings and sleepy

rains.

Summer is awfully cheery for too good a

reason.

Fall is when I come alive; it's my best

season.

Lamont L. Nance

Shelter

Our truest failure is displacing the rock in
our lives.
We become small as an excuse.
Forget that nothingness is a weight none can
carry
In the loneliest of hours it is there for you –
Within the pit of your stomach, that chip
upon your shoulder.
Perhaps a rock and a hard place will help
you survive the storm.

Lamont L. Nance

Shoelaces

When words aren't enough
And nothing done goes right
There is a summit unreached.

Often we wonder about love
The reasons that go unexplained
And why the silences between are long.

What we once thought small
Were the fault lines ignored
The moments never returned

We forget the why of it all
Why we hold it so dear
And give in good faith.

For the quiet to be worn easy
The need to upturn rocks must be settled
Lest we find no end to the noise.

To be sure is a journey
Arrived at when all is lost
When life is ashen and threadbare.

Age doesn't ensure wisdom
Loving doesn't mean you'll be loved
And hoping doesn't guarantee solace.

If we are lucky enough
We will rise from night's bed
Put on shoes and tie the laces

Uncertainty is our shadow.

Spectrums

Why can't sunlight perceive the layers
hidden away?
See me in infrared and my anger will blind
you.
Stick to the shadows and I am a ghost.
Shine me in black light to view the stain of
my failures.
Don't look into the darkness – my wounds
are legion.
See me in ultra violet and notice the bonds
that tether me.
Witness me in starlight for a glimpse of my
mountainous soul.
In candlelight, look at me so I can see you
too. And what does moonlight reveal? The
same thing it does of you.

Lamont L. Nance

Stand and Be Counted

In times of distress we wonder about legacy,

Ponder forays into the dangerous and

distraught

Of this life complicated by us.

If we're to discern what matters,

isn't it important to be sure of the

answers we give?

Should an indelible imprint blind us

from the everyday civilities which

engender the security of commonality?

We have in common the Earth and

our humanity. What responses are

we giving the grass in our wake to

those who follow?

Our greatest impression should be

forerunning.

Lamont L. Nance

Super Nova

Heaviness leveled in tiers.

They mirror nothing like new canvas.

Banded together and resistant to

exposure.

Impression.

Stains.

Trussed and hung like garlic.

Anticipatory within me.

Brindled the deeper one delves.

Darkness.

A darkness worthy of communion.

Made like rails fashioned for trains.

Seducing me. Roaring.

Scouring and blindingly silent.

Careening to smash and explode.

Chemical synthesis.

Triturated.

And blown away for the Becoming.

I have removed every aspect.

My bandages shorn.

For those depths found remiss.

To love.

To live brilliant.

Brighter than any light guiding the
lost home.

Immense like pressure upon the wind.

Retained.

A road of unending darkness.

To be courageous for the traveling.

Serialize me as nothing and nobody.

Companion in shadow.

Eternal waif.

With temerity, a flicker.

A rising each day to love the Night
within.

Teenage Angst

Yesterday the Moon was full – monsoon
deep and vast.
Like the irritatingly needed breath when
kissing your lips.
Lips sweeter than revenge, tongue cherry
red and tangy.

On edge while strummed taunt – as the steps
you take lightly—
Body curved/interstate/wound tightly/jack-
in-the-box/popped.
Crisp autumnal moon bliss for a wonder at
Summer's ardent kiss.

I wonder/wonder/wonder/wonder for an
instance remiss –

Wonder what it was like to miss the signs
given –
When I opened my eyes to see yours looking
back at me – I didn't understand.

There is No Lake Here

I walk in circles

Like a six foot hamster

Within miles of razor wire

And walls that suffocate the stars.

Around and around I go

Through seasons and years

Cried rivers and ignited darkness.

There is no lake here.

My bastion, Michigan, I miss you.

Lamont L. Nance

Three Types

I walk in silence

My mind empty

My soul pure

My spirit austere

My essence a void

I live in silence

For the trees

For the expanses of untouched snow

For those crypts never found

For a deep trench far below

I am silent

Because there are no words to express

Because there is a mountain in my

heart

Because there were moments too loud

Because right now you need me to be.

Lamont L. Nance

Today in this World

In this world I am epic—beyond awesome. Legendary. Label me warrior, thief, assassin and sword magus. I thought of becoming a cleric, but I'm not devout enough for some God to claim me. Besides, alignments don't matter. I've traveled too many planes to count, pillaged hundreds of coffers, and looted a few dragon hordes to boot.

I am the knight of the meridian, prince of the horizon, lord of shadowy tavern corners and lover of bar maids. I am the Knave Supreme! Bane of abyssal demons and infernal devils! Enemy of several nations and savior to a dozen more. I even have my own quintet of bards.

I recall traumatic experiences with a mind-probing squid over a jibe about seafood and being hounded to the deepest levels of the underground, where chaos touches reality, by an inconsolable Arch Lich claiming I stole his ladylove. Four centuries ago, no less! Those individuals were far too serious. I cannot imagine such a dross existence without the joy of a good fight, laughing at my own blunders at the fire with companions, and ale, lots of ale.

I have seen Gods battle and world-bending powers fail. Even a beardless dwarf, much to my dismay. Did you know that they look exceedingly young beneath those beards? Almost a child with eyes too knowing. Scary.

Today I barely got away from a fiendish giant warmonger named Bramble Dreadfoot. His feet reeked, so I zapped him in the face with a lightning bolt and tangled his legs with vines. Nasty business it was…smelly too. Today, in this world, I'm a freaking beast! Tomorrow, well, tomorrow I go back to work like everyone else. But next week the twenty die will roll again.

Lamont L. Nance

To Glitter

For something often believed too much or gaudy when placed in contrast to the somber and stuffiness of those who conform, whose only want is to be the same so that they won't be left out. Left out of everything and nothing since it is all the same anyway. Left free from feeling themselves completely.

I ask that you surge against the tide, spread your wings and soar over the contemporaries, and view the breadth of this life to embrace its limitlessness. Believe that being you, unequivocally and selflessly, is the most important gift that you can give to this world. Doing this, you will glitter brighter than an ocean of diamonds that won't hurt the eyes.

Lamont L. Nance

To Know Why

I walk until walking is the only notion my

spirit understands. All my mind is aware of.

Much

like I've spent my entire life. Oblivious.

Through

Love. Glimmers of Hatred. Through the

skeins of Hope.

Trekked on despite the near insurmountable

hills of

Disappointment. I walked through the field

of shards

that remained of Happiness. Stepped

beyond the burning

Plateau of Need and the razored precipice of

Certainty.

Charred and in ribbons, I walked on.

I went until I met Misery in the woods and

then, together, that phantom Despair with a

pot on

a fire beside a creek. Cups were provided. I

shared

in the lavender and spruce tea with them, as

they proved

to be good company and understood me a

great deal. We

spoke through the day. Discerned that we

were just

motes in the sand, how walking required so

much from

the spirit. How with them. I could allay

myself of

this burden without judgment.

I was weary, the tea delicious, and

something

in their eyes comforted sweetly. Knew. I

could stay

they said. But I itched. I had to keep going.

So,

I bid them fair skies and strove forth across

the flatland

of Optimism carrying them in my heart.

Clouds striated

the sky in hues of grace, tranquility and

something

Fey. Night petitioned.

In the darkest of hours I crawled through

briars

of Self-doubt, grew lost within the endless

caverns

of Ego, walked in the rain of Joy to find a

rainbow

of Solace over an arctic chasm of Anger and

Impotency.

I walked and experienced mountain ranges

of Loss, crossed

the river Confusion only to meet a sea of

Disillusionment

which led to my submersion within that

vastly bleak

ocean Depression.

From that abyss I emerged broken and

scarred,

knowing Dysfunction intimately, pulled on

by the claws

of Desperation in hunger for something

more. Feral

and obsolete, I shuffled into the Saltlands

surrounded

by cacti and the skeletal remains of lives

taken for

granted.

On into the distance I walked, as the land

became unfettered, dry and withered as

Emaciation wracked

me with its severity. In that scattered

desolation

a patience barred my progression. Quietus.

With a

spectral finger my attention was drawn to a

cricket.

It said it was about to be reaped. The ground

near

the Pedestrian screamed, exploding in a

black crunch

as it was dragged into a hidden hold.

Trapdoor spider.

A different emptiness rocked me observing

that passing

of ethereal sustenance. Visions of circles

and the

settlement of scales filled what could

comprehend in

my mind. I was permitted to leave

understanding that

I wasn't next. Yet.

Numb, I barely recognized that my lungs

and

olfactory senses no longer burned or

struggled to take

in air, that, the ground was softer and easier

upon

the knees.

It squished. Moss grew upon rocks, patches

and splotches of green grassy microhills

towered over

footsized puddles. Grasshoppers sang of

Desire. Clouds

of gnats tied into knotted bowties.

Marshland.

I was thirsty. Hungry. Still I walked.

Haze brained, I fell face first. Wetness

greeted

me. I gorged. Something akin to chimes and

the witnessing

of a blossoming caressed me. Soothed.

Graphed together.

A tiny figure sat upon the microhill before

me attending

a pole and line. The scent of living things

and freshly

churned soil resurrected my being. Life

welcomed me

with a beatific smile, offered fish, some

bread, and

honeyed tea from its satchel.

Encouragement. Satisfaction.

Its expression was most curious for the

Vulnerable

wonderment I found therein. I grew unsure

because

of the sanctity within it. For the first time in

my

existence I was looked at like I mattered. *As*

if I

were utterly beautiful. My vision grew

blurry. I

cried the tears of a lifetime. I was alone,

when my

eyes cleared, filled with a Solitude long

achieved

by redwood giants and the silence of empty

rooms neither

vacant nor longing. Just loved.

Onward my feet took me through water to

my

shins that dried away as the land flattened.

Swaying

gold rippled as the wind rolled through the

wheat plain.

The smell of contentment baked and sliced

settled in

my core. Left me warm. I bounced as birds

marked

my passage and the Sun born full. For miles

I placed

a step afore the other.

A sudden roaring pressured the World.

Squeezed

to break it. A concentrated dirge of several

voices

not dominating. Pure. Bright. Colossal. An

insidious

blight corrosive to being filled the skyline.

The

hydra Fear. Each of its unmerciful heads

was an aurora

Borealis that pulsated vitriol in waves that

saturated,

corrupted and destroyed the ground. Its

roiling breath

seared a requiem.

Almost comically, a black armored figure

behind

shield withstood. Its sword a hungry void.

Shadows

lengthened defiantly. A dark warping

surged, spiked

into the air around the knave. Courage, that

lone

forgotten sentinel. Primordial forces reared.

Vapors

and bars of Light clashed with millions of

filaments

of Darkness, which birthed striated gray

pillars that stabbed

into The Place That Was Not A Place. The

universe strobed

and shook as they battled. I ran to get away.

My jaunt led to a forest where I stumbled

and

fell, was lacerated by branches and thorns,

resisted

against by brush and vines. Each step

produced increasingly

haunting images of twisted caricatures

struggling to

escape their personal hell. There was no

wind. Just

a stillness that left my soul feeling damned.

Forgotten.

Forsaken.

Encircled within a pristine clearing, a

humanoid

shaped mound sat in its center. Its form was

twisted

and melded together as if by some

incandescence that

couldn't conceive beyond its brutal

perspective of

rightness. Hopelessness and Sadness.

Conjoined twins

regal in all their dismay.

Their eyes rested upon me dull and piercing.

Aggressive. In that instance of brushing

minds I found

myself assailed.   Bent low and bowed by

the magnitude

of their presence, which bombarded with its

suffocating

nihilism. The nexus of who I've known

myself to be

splintered as thin ice does beneath heavy

steps, flaked

and shed away like dead skin. Blown like so

much dust

in a gale. My Will Was Shorn.

Those flecks swirled and darted like protons,

refashioned themselves in rebellion only to

shatter

before imploding. A void opened that wasn't

and was

me. Left me hollow. A receptacle for the

maelstrom

of Misconception. A convoluted and frantic

voice stabbed

through to me, dictating that it will all be for

nothing

in the end. Insisted there was no true value

in walking

since it took instead of gave. Demanded that

I sit

and become triune. That I take up the mantle

of Apathy.

Told me that I wouldn't have to *care*

anymore. About

Walking. About being. Reminded me that I

was tired.

A sudden weariness overwhelmed me to the

bone,

spreading as water hyacinth does in late

spring. Just

sit that voice roared. Sit. My knees buckled.

I had

to use a hand to catch myself. For the first

time

in my life, I was weak, more alone than I

had ever

recalled. I felt the storm ripping me apart.

Another voice spoke to me. It was

measured.

Filled with an ease that beleaguered sailors

found in

the Eye and immediately drew my attention.

There is

so much to give yet, that voice said, you can

overcome

Being weary. My name is Help. I am here.

At those words something shifted inside me,

a new facet shined. Calmness reverberated

like the

thrumming of a harpsichord within a

marbled room. There

was no ceiling and I felt boundless. *Someone*

cared.

Mustering a kernel, I made a nugget, from a

nugget

I developed a cube. A cube veered into a

bar, that

bar fashioned itself into a beam and that

beam into a wall.

I made that wall hard. Harder than the

acceptance

of bitter truths generations inbred. A focal

point

to stake my humanity upon. Arduously, I reclaimed

myself. Worn. Patchworked.

The storm in my head whined, gathered in streaks

of crimson and viridian Lightning which boiled and

seethed around a pillar of gray light. It was Help.

I stepped into it and was embraced as a fetus is.

Rising to my feet, I rejected the twins.

Annealed I walked out of the forest bolstered;

pushed through the dense foliage out into a sunlit

vista. A sparkling winding river stretched

for miles

into the distance. Hills dotted the horizon; a

pathway

woven between them.

Birds soared amongst the clouds and zebras

galloped playfully. Antelope grazed while

elephants

trumpeted water into the sky like a prayer.

The wind

brought a cool breeze carrying the

symphonic music

of leaves. A feeling of communion instilled

the moment.

I felt a sense of renewal through the earth

reaching

up and into me. Everything was brilliant.

Beautifully

itself. This was Peace given flesh.

Two beings arrived, one to each side of me,

and overlooked the landscape in

companionable silence.

Wisdom and Mercy. That they were present

felt natural.

Right. Mercy smiled at me, reached over

and held my

hand. In that touch, my painful and troubled

reality

meant nothing as a healing warmth seeped

inside me.

Permeated like a balm soothing burned skin.

There

was no need for words.

Wisdom turned to me with eyes infinite and

knowing. Compassionate. Then pointed

behind me.

Turning, I witnessed a multitude stepping

clear of

the forest line. They looked tired and tried.

Beat

but unbeaten. They had followed me. My

heart swelled.

I was amazed by their fortitude and felt a

kinship

with them all. Many embraced me and soon

I was encircled.

There were tears and thanks and knowing

looks. More

tears. Their gratitude drowned me. I had

never been

more grateful in my life.

Over the hum I remembered Wisdom

saying. Being

surefooted starts with accepting uncertainty.

The

journey of one's life is to cherish the

distance and

value the walk itself. Should you not be

sensible

about this truth, Perseverance, a single step

can

and will encourage thousands to be brave

enough to

take theirs. This is why you do it.

And I have been walking ever since.

To View the Night

There where the sand can be white between
toes…
to be there.
For silence within conjoinment ….
while the sun sets as birds sing away their
woes.

To witness the horizon become indigo …
to leave it behind.
Again and again … to shine.
No clouds to block a sequined night of belit
purple.

A reminder of joy derived from a silvered
face …
nothing to want.

What hoped for kept …

To breathe as finger-locked hands.

For a glance beyond, to embrace repeatedly

…

searching the night for the Sentinel.

Beseeching.

And build the bridge to attune with Grace.

Crystal fulminations, of blue, illume the

aeroscape …

waiting.

For the orb.

Within the heart roll shadowed filaments,

made tangible with love;

From and back despite unending miles …

harvester and crescented.

Unveiled.

Beholden to many though seldom touched;

Calling tides and combers of waves…

surpassing the Heavens.

A shifting of facets.

To tend a garden upon the moon.

Lamont L. Nance

Turpentine

I wish for words to say
What I never could
That my actions were able
To reaffirm the things that I should.
For there will be moments
Remembered that leave me
Wishing that I would
Have that silence from yesterday
Returned to strip away
The layers now between us.

Lamont L. Nance

Untitled I

Before the sun refashions itself and awakens

the world

It is dark somewhere because the night is

vast

And I can leave behind the frailties of the

day

Dappled shadows kiss my lacquered sky

black

Beneath the stars I come alive

As if some cosmic synergism ignites me

I can dwell within the night sky forever

Look at my silvered cloak wrought of

moonlight

The stardust obscuring the universes in my

veins

I eat and drink from the dippers

I walk with Orion's belt upon my waist

Saturn's rings my bandolier and Jupiter a

bowling ball

During eventide I swim the Milky Way

At midnight I lunch amongst the Zodiac

In the darkest hour I sup within black holes

My night's wondrous from the back porch

My soul voyages the deepest space

My mind the bridge of impassable gaps

Vigil

It is peculiar to reflect on your life and understand that you know so very little about yourself. For years I have been good and struggled to live good in the stead of another, but have felt unfulfilled and disjointed as if I had no roots. No thing to anchor me. Nothing to prevent the Mack truck of my guilt from dragging me by chain down a back road...

What I realized today was that I don't know what it means to live for me. Robert Frost spoke about a fork in the road-a choosing of a path... and not worrying overly much because (this is all my interpretation), all of these roads are the same and how we perceive them determines our course. When we think poorly we do poorly. Just as if we hinder what is life giving in our lives, we allow what drains us to affect everything we love for the worse.

I cannot tell you enough how living uncertain and in ignorance, can leave you like chaff and unfruitful, feeling as if all of your efforts are for nothing.

What I have come to understand about this vigil, about myself, is that I cannot live for anyone if I cannot live for myself. I cannot love. I cannot bear fruit. I cannot be what I know myself to be or who everyone that loves me knows me to be. I have been living without hope.

I make no declarations. Rather I will just share with you that I am choosing to live with hope. Bear fruit. Understand that ignorance has many shades. Most importantly, that forgiveness is for oneself as well. That it is a constant process and only then will I have the life I want to have.

Peace favor you....

Lamont L. Nance

Wake Up

I was told too many things tend to be
hard to carry at once,
that a man's shoulders weren't meant
to carry the entire world.
Then why are women doing it every single
day?

Lamont L. Nance

Wings

I have wings made of shadow

So I do not fly,

Instead they scale the walls

Of my cell, counting the bars

Upon the window, the notches

In the steel door, the many

Coats of paint hiding the misery

Of millennia staining this world.

I have wings made of shadow

And they are restless

Because nothing I do satiates

Them. In the light they

Burn away like fog in summer.

I have wings made of shadow

And when it is dark I soar the

Universe—free from this, free

As the blue finch dreaming about pound

cake and

New York vanilla ice cream and

Quiet evenings with the shade of my heart.

I have wings of shadow and it is count time

again…

Wordless

I don't really know what to say

or really what to express ever

to you

myself

to anyone at all.

Everything is just a smattering of words

dashed upon the walls like soup

like pasta burned on the bottom of a pot.

Our skulls resemble those things

heads rolling.

If you don't look too far into it

fragile instances will pass you by

until the floor of reality greets you.

Isn't that what life should be?

Perpetual wonderment about why?

What life shouldn't be yesterday …

staying forever today within old summers

young winter afternoons in shorts.

Moments ignored playing football

remembering nothing

Thought-less.

None of us really want to share anything

say anything.

Rather do something...

anything but reveal to you.

How sad is that?

I guess I really don't have anything to say.

Wanna play catch?

You Are Something

Something about waking up to you
motivates—sends me bumble bee buzzing
along through the din of rush hour traffic—
happy.

Something about you is like walking
beneath dappled autumn leaves holding
hands, or splashing sandaled feet through
water.

You are life-altering. Words will never do
you justice.

Lamont L. Nance

Author's Endnote

I share these thoughts with you, dear reader, in the hope that they remind you of where you felt more at peace and where you have garnered more of yourself. I also hope that I have made some sense to you and that you have learned a little about me.

Lamont L. Nance

Songs from the Shadows

Lamont L. Nance

Songs from the Shadows

Made in the USA
Columbia, SC
19 February 2020